BLISSFUL JOURNEY

5 STEPS ON YOUR PATH TO BLISS

BELLA ROHATGI

A Book By:
FOREVER SHININGS
Instagram - @forevershinings.co
www.forevershinings.com

Book Title: Blissful Journey

Book Author: Bella Rohatgi

Published By: FOREVER SHININGS

ISBN: 978-93-5605-318-2

I Invoke My Blessings To Lord Krishna

Five Steps On Your Path To Bliss

About the Author

The author is deeply dedicated to uplifting others, guided by the profound belief that God resides in every heart. Heaven is on this earth where we have taken birth .A self-motivated and goal-oriented academician, she brings years of rich experience as a mentor and guide to countless children, inspiring them to pursue purposeful lives and charting paths toward goal-oriented careers. Her compassion extends beyond the classroom—she runs a school for underprivileged children, driven by her mission to empower the community in her own meaningful way. Through her work, she aspires to transform lives and nurture brighter futures.

With her experience of over 20 years she aims to create inclusive learning environments and empowering underprivileged communities through education. With a passion for teaching and a commitment to social change, she actively engages in initiatives that promote literacy, skill development, and personal growth. Her work reflects a deep understanding of the diverse needs of children and a strong belief in the power of education to transform lives.

This is her second book . First one is titled – Peace on your Platter.

ABOUT THE BOOK

Blissful Journey invites readers to rediscover the beauty of life, even amidst its challenges. Through thoughtful reflections and inspiring insights, the book emphasizes the importance of facing life's ups and downs with courage, self-control, and resilience. It explores the significance of personal growth, staying fit and healthy, and embracing every stage of life with grace and positivity. Rooted in faith and prayer, this journey encourages readers to nurture a deep connection with God, finding strength and peace in His presence. Whether you're seeking motivation, guidance, or a fresh perspective, Blissful Journey is a heartfelt companion on your path to a fulfilling life.

A book that will truly inspire and uplift readers.

INTRODUCTION

The goal of writing this book is to guide readers to a happy life that promotes self-growth, community involvement, and a peaceful lifestyle. This vision can potentially encourage readers to pursue personal pleasure while also making a constructive contribution to their surroundings. I believe there is a great need to delve deep within and find peace while enjoying life's path joyfully.

This book teaches how to live with love, serenity, and contentment. There will be ups and downs, but we must face them without fear, hate, hatred, or despair to grow. I've shared several experiences from my life in my last book, so if you haven't read it yet, maybe this will inspire you to do so. I would be overjoyed if my words might make some difference in readers' lives.

I am grateful to my readers who ponder on the purpose and connect with the sentiments in a conscious and caring way, promoting a life of joy, self-improvement, and community connection. Self-improvement is not a one-time event; it is a way of life. Self-improvement is a very personal and transforming journey that requires a commitment to growth and a desire to achieve deeper self-awareness. Self-awareness is the foundation of this journey because it allows us to comprehend our thoughts, emotions, and motives, which leads to more deliberate decisions.

Goals that are consistent with your basic beliefs might help you feel a sense of purpose and influence your activities. Regularly imagine who you want to become, attempting to understand your mission.

"Spread love everywhere you go. Let no one ever come to you without leaving happier."

—Mother Teresa

DEDICATION

I'm thankful to God and the universe for giving me the understanding to compose this book and make a little attempt to make this world more joyful. Every effort matters. I'm appreciative to my whole family for empowering me throughout my excursions and encounters. I am extremely grateful to my parents for imparting values that I can share.

I would like to express my gratitude to Jatin Sir for his workshop, which pushed me to complete my work.

I would like to extend my thanks to the Publisher for making it available in the market, and a special thank you to all of the readers for bringing peace into their daily lives. I hope you enjoy the information and put the recommendations into action.

I will always hold a special place in my heart for all those people who have always been with me through my life journey and have made a difference in my life, who have helped in making me what I am today for their love and good wishes.

CONTENTS

CHAPTER : 1
FACING LIFE CHALLENGES

"Where there is no struggle, there is no strength."
– Oprah Winfrey

Life isn't without its storms. From the minute we take our first breath, we enter a world full of joy, conflict, success, and trial. Challenges can take various forms, some of which we anticipate, while others catch us off guard like unexpected gusts of wind. We all had various experiences. We tend to remember some experiences while forgetting others. I would describe each day of our lives as a miraculous journey. We choose many paths, some difficult and rough, some straight and easy going. When we walk simply and straight, we are at ease; nevertheless, this comfort zone causes us to become complacent. We must all work hard and make progress.

Overcoming Obstacles:

Our response to problems is what defines us, not the obstacles themselves. Every adversity has a lesson, an opportunity to become stronger, smarter, and more resilient. However, the process of accepting these lessons is rarely simple. It takes guts, patience, and a willingness to face the discomfort of change. To progress, we must overcome our difficulties and challenge them on our own.

Moving On in Life: The key to overcoming and forgetting barriers is to recognize that moving forward is essential for overcoming life's challenges and that dwelling on the past can stifle personal growth.

In childhood, I was a headstrong girl, especially when my parents chastised me. I'd spend the entire day, if not longer, thinking about it and not talking to them, which irritated them. We did not grasp other people's feelings as children. I am sure many of us behave in the same way because we take others for granted, particularly our parents. I apologize to them for their behaviour, which resulted in the rundown. A parent's love is unconditional, and they continually forgive their offspring. As I grew older and faced fresh challenges in my life, I learned a lot while also changing my way of thinking. I prayed that the issues I was experiencing would not be shared by anybody else, particularly a female who is transitioning from the coziness and comforts of her home to a completely new world with unfamiliar people. Every family has unique ways of thinking, working, eating, and much more. However, the girl is required to shift her mindset and adapt to the new environment. I somehow managed to avoid holding any grudges toward anyone. I then recognized that every problem serves as a learning opportunity. So we must take each experience positively.

It is necessary to confront unpleasant conditions. Each challenge helps us grow stronger and more experienced. The next time we encounter the same difficulty, we will come out much more prepared since we will have a solution or approach for dealing with it. Accepting the truth of a situation is the first step toward overcoming it. Moving on frequently enhances relationships, allowing us to approach others without the burden of previous frustrations.

I am immensely grateful to God for keeping me joyful and teaching me the value of every person in our lives. They are there to teach us something, whether or not we enjoy their presence.

Some individuals teach us patience, some modifications, and some are there to help us understand how to compromise, they give us the courage to face challenges or they teach us organization and systematic working, discipline, and various other characteristics if we are observant. Throughout my life, I've come to understand that we can't change another person's conduct, attitude, or thinking. However, we can either cast or depict our behaviours in front of them, as parents did before their kids, to serve as role models for them in their days or we may allow them to be themselves and progress. In this big globe, it's tough to please everyone. It is better to know the understanding to accept what we cannot change while changing what we can to MOVE ON regularly.

When interacting with others, we often get a sense of their personality and whether they exude positivity or negativity. We naturally feel drawn to like-minded individuals, while those with contrasting traits may seem more challenging to connect with. It is commonly believed that positive and disciplined individuals attract people with similar characteristics. However, in reality, we frequently encounter individuals with opposing traits, especially among those close to us. While we may not be able to change them, we can learn to coexist, adapt, and even grow from these differences. Though this is often easier said than done, for the sake of our mental peace, it is essential to accept people as they are and choose to live joyfully.

How to Thrive Through Life's Challenges

Even situations might be either advantageous or unfavourable. For example, if you are dissatisfied with your job or a member of your family becomes ill, you must confront the situation fearlessly and seek assistance if needed. If you are unable to find adequate guidance, the supreme power is the ultimate solution. We sincerely ask God to guide us down the right road. If we are unable to make a critical decision, we can pray to God for guidance on the best way for us.

All of the senior members of our family, particularly my father and father-in-law, believed in simple living high thinking'. They had only the necessary stuff in their cabinets and were orderly and organized. This aided them in their basic daily requirements. They were disciplined, punctual, and careful in all of their endeavours. Life's obstacles can be readily overcome if we execute our task with honesty. Things are automatically sorted out.
They have taught me many facets of living a healthy, conscientious, stress-free life. They say that if you keep laughing, it relieves stress and makes it easier to handle any obstacles.

I used to have a home assistant who had two girls and one boy. She had lost her spouse but was working for her own survival and raising her children with the help of her brother. One day, her older daughter in class X received her board results and did not pass. As a result, she became extremely upset and resolved to terminate her life. But, fortunately, her mother arrived home in time and saved her. This girl felt awful about her incompetence and chose to retake the course. This time, she worked hard and finished her assignments.

Later, she completed her XII grade and began attending computer programs to strengthen her abilities while still taking language courses. That one setback transformed her life. She began setting higher ambitions, demonstrating how failures and obstacles make us stronger.

Do not blame God when you fail or face a terrible scenario. Rather, praise him for bringing you closer to him, since you pray with sincerity and faith. **"joy is the interval between two pains, while pain is the interval between two joys"** highlights the cyclical nature of life. Just as happiness is temporary, so is suffering—both are inevitable and alternate over time. This mirrors the rhythm of breathing, which moves up and down, symbolizing the natural flow of life's ups and downs.

Ultimately, the message is to embrace life's fluctuations with faith and resilience, knowing that neither joy nor pain is permanent, and both contribute to personal growth.

Stories about Survival and Growth

Steve Jobs' life is a fascinating story of perseverance, tenacity, and visionary development. Here's a quick peek at his journey:

Steve Jobs was born in 1955 and adopted shortly after that. Jobs' adoptive parents were sympathetic, but he struggled academically and often felt detached. Regardless, he developed a strong interest in electronics and technology. After quitting out of Reed College in Portland, Oregon, Jobs searched for his purpose. He experimented with spiritual travels and uncommon interests, such as traveling to India to study Zen Buddhism.

Jobs and his friend Steve Wozniak launched Apple Inc. in their parents' garage in 1976. Their first device, the Apple I, sold moderately, but the Apple II transformed the personal computer business. The company flourished swiftly, and Jobs, then in his early twenties, became a multimillionaire. However, the success did not last long. After a series of disagreements over the company's direction, Jobs was pushed to leave Apple in 1985 by the executives he had hired.

Being fired from Apple was one of the most painful events of Jobs' life. Instead of giving up, he used the opportunity to reflect, grow, and build. Jobs launched a new company, NeXT, which specializes in high-end workstations for universities and companies. Though NeXT was not a major commercial success, the technologies it built would go on to play an important part in shaping Apple's future.

Apple acquired NeXT in 1997, bringing Jobs back to the business he co-founded, as it struggled with dwindling sales and innovation. His comeback signalled a new era for Apple. Jobs took daring steps, streamlined the company's product portfolio, and produced ground-breaking devices including the iMac, iPod, iPhone, and iPad. These products transformed various industries, including computing, music, mobile phones, and entertainment.

In 2003, Jobs was diagnosed with a rare type of pancreatic cancer. He originally refused regular medical treatments, preferring alternative alternatives, but eventually underwent surgery. Despite battling the illness for several years, Jobs led Apple through some of its most prosperous years. In 2011, due to declining health, he stepped down as CEO.

Jobs passed away in October 2011, leaving behind an incredible legacy. He was a visionary leader, a brilliant marketer, and a relentless innovator whose ideas shaped the modern world.

Another such example is the story of J K Rowling

J.K. Rowling: From Rejection to Global Success

J.K. Rowling, the world-famous author of the *Harry Potter* series, faced extreme hardship before her success. After her mother died from multiple sclerosis, Rowling moved to Portugal to teach English, but her marriage failed, leaving her a single mother struggling with depression. She returned to the UK, jobless and relying on government assistance, writing her now-famous novel in cafes while caring for her daughter.

Despite facing multiple rejections from publishers, Rowling persisted. It wasn't until Bloomsbury agreed to publish her book, thanks to the encouragement of the CEO's young daughter, that *Harry Potter* became a reality. The series went on to sell over 500 million copies, transforming Rowling from a struggling single mother into one of the most successful authors in the world. Her journey is a testament to resilience, persistence, and the power of believing in one's dreams.

Failures do come our way as I said ups and downs are a way of life. Do not run away keep looking for opportunities and new experiences for personal and professional growth. Look for something that you like. Love what you do-keep focusing on who you are now and who you want to become. You become what you think. Have faith and move on. Believe in the Divine power.

Remember :

I am willing to accept – what God Almighty has given me
I am willing to give – to the community in whatever way I can
I am willing to receive – whatever is in store for me with God's will

CHAPTER : 2

SELF-CONTROL-MINDFULNESS

I cannot always control what goes on outside. But I can always control what goes on inside.

-Wayne Dyer

Balance between actions and emotions is a critical component of existence. We may control all of our activities. The mind's work is most important. Our emotions, behaviour, and habits—particularly those related to eating, sleeping, and speaking—are among the most important components of our existence.

As a child, I was a temperamental girl, but with time I realized that mood swings may be readily changed. It is as simple as turning on and off the light and fan buttons. We only need to identify the cause of our negative mood. A little mental activity can lift our spirits from low to high. Perhaps self-introspection or self-talk might easily shift our focus.

When we focus on the now, we release the weight of the past and the concerns of the future. Simple pleasures like as watching the setting sun, listening to birdsong, or enjoying a cup of coffee help us stay present.

Control of Language

Words are among the most powerful instruments we have. They have the ability to create or destroy, heal or harm, motivate or discourage. The words we use not only reflect who we are but also shape those around us and the world we live in. Being attentive of the influence of our words can result in more meaningful, productive, and happy encounters.

The Power of Words

Words have the power to inspire, heal, motivate, and transform lives. They can bring hope in times of despair, encouragement in moments of doubt, and comfort in times of sorrow. A kind word can uplift someone's spirit, while a harsh one can break a heart.

Words shape our thoughts, influence our emotions, and define our relationships. They can start wars or bring peace, create love or spread hatred. The way we use our words determines their impact—whether they build bridges or burn them.

Choosing our words wisely is essential, as they leave lasting impressions. Speaking with kindness, truth, and wisdom can make a difference, not just in our own lives but in the lives of those around us. After all, words are not just sounds or letters—they carry energy, meaning, and power. The importance of words and their impact extends across various aspects of life, including personal interactions, professional communication, and self-expression Well-chosen words can inspire people to act, set objectives, or make beneficial changes.

Great leaders and presenters utilize words to motivate and guide others.

Controlling language and being attentive to your words is critical since once stated, it cannot be undone. Here are some **tips for managing your words** and communicating more successfully.

'Think before you speak' is a familiar adage. Take a moment before answering, especially in emotionally charged circumstances where someone is furious or upset. This pause can help you avoid saying something you later regret. Drink water, go around in the fresh air, and then Ask yourself: Is it true? Is this necessary? Is it kind? These questions can help you formulate your response. You will notice that your attitude will change, many times we look at the situation from a different angle or the issue causing chaos in our mind takes a U-turn and our response becomes accepted or agreeable by others. In heated moments, keeping your tone calm can prevent a situation from escalating.

Instead of pointing out problems or criticizing, try to reframe statements in a constructive, solution-oriented way. Avoid negative triggers: Certain words or phrases can escalate conflicts. Avoid accusatory language like "you always" or "you never." Even if you're frustrated, choosing words that don't insult or belittle others is important.

Sometimes regulating your words entails saying less and listening more. This allows you to act appropriately, avoid assumptions, and exhibit respect for others. Before replying, demonstrate empathy and consider how the other person is feeling.

Use "I" comments (for example, "I feel upset when...") rather than "You" remarks, which might sound accusatory and put others on the defensive. If you say something hurtful, acknowledge it right away and apologize. If you are misunderstood, clarify your intention and intent to avoid further injury.

Find nice things to say about individuals and situations. Regularly express gratitude and appreciation for others' efforts or actions. Being thoughtful in your choice of words and accepting responsibility for what you say helps create stronger relationships, avoid misunderstandings, and maintain a sense of peace and respect in your communications.

Every morning, my husband and I go for a walk through the park and stop at a small temple in one corner. After prayer, we frequently meet a gardener/caretaker who takes excellent care of the property. He shows us the fresh plants he brings and how he takes care of them. As we express our interest in him, a few words of conversation bring him joy and demonstrate his enthusiasm for his work. It's not about how well you know someone, but about how you communicate, your body language, and compassion.

Every parent must create the practice of speaking well and positively about others in front of their children. Never grumble or argue since parents are responsible for teaching their children the joys of life. This makes them happy as individuals.

On the other hand, negative, critical, or discouraging comments can demotivate and hinder individuals from acting, sometimes rendering them averse to change or advancement. A person's words influence how others perceive them. Consistently employing gentle, thoughtful language fosters a reputation for dependability, whereas thoughtless or cruel language harms one's image. The manner you communicate reflects your values, views, and personality. Words containing respect, honesty, and empathy demonstrate a person's positive attributes. I discovered that if you accidentally say the incorrect words, you must quickly seek forgiveness in your heart so that the other person's feelings are not wounded.

Speaking with arrogance reflects the speaker's character rather than the listener's. The words we utter to ourselves influence our internal dialogue. Positive self-talk promotes self-belief. Gives us the confidence and guts to accept.

Control of personal habits: especially eating and sleeping.

I often believe that it is critical to control our eating habits. Maintaining excellent health requires control over one's food choices. We must plan what, how much, and when we consume. A well-balanced nutritional intake improves overall health and weight maintenance.

Many folks crave sweets. I'm also one of them. We just say, "I have a sweet tooth," but I know that if I choose not to eat sweets, I can control my cravings. We often find alternatives, but the best option is to limit your quantities or use portion control. Remind yourself of what is healthy for you and what is not.

Treat food as sacred, acknowledging the effort, natural resources, and life that go into each meal. Eating with reverence honours the holy energy contained in food, developing gratitude and attentiveness. This method encourages us to slow down, enjoy each bite, and nourish both our bodies and our spirits.

If you find it difficult to regulate specific eating habits on your own, consult with a nutritionist or therapist who specializes in eating behaviours.

Sleeping late at night is a typical tendency among young people. However, this breaks the morning routine of waking up early, preferably before sunrise, and working on yourself. As we get older, we settle into a defined routine of day and night. The energy we receive from the early light benefits our entire system, which is why God created day and night.

We may easily set our body cycle in accordance with the cosmos if we comprehend its relevance. The morning sets the tone for the day, invigorating and priming you for success. It promotes a positive mindset and attention.

Work on yourself.

Begin the day with prayer and exercise. Making time for yourself is one of the most important things you can do for your health, development, and enjoyment. When you devote time to self-care and reflection, you make room to recharge, better understand yourself, and meet your own needs. This results in a better grasp of your goals, values, and priorities, making it easier to live in accordance with them.

When you care for yourself, you are better able to support and interact with others. Taking time for yourself allows you to create appropriate boundaries, communicate better, and bring more patience and understanding to your relationships.

Being completely conscious of who we are--our attitude, conduct, speech, and body language--helps to improve our overall health. Physical and mental. Practice thoughtful activities such as deep breathing, yoga, or mindful walking.

Take time to reflect on your actions, decisions, and emotions. Understand your feelings. Internal growth is a lifelong journey. Learn from each one in every situation. Focus on solutions instead of problems.

Once, husband and wife had an altercation in which each blamed the other for being overburdened with labour. The wife had domestic chores in addition to her office work, and her husband was unable to assist due to his hectic schedule. This type of difference is frequent in all families. The remedy lies in our words and in improving ourselves so that the conflicts can be reconciled. Respecting the other person and focusing on the root cause of the problem can quickly resolve the situation. They can both sit down and share their duties, as well as express gratitude and apologize, which can lead to a better understanding.

SEE THE BEST AND IGNORE THE REST.

If we don't focus on the other person's flaws and instead look for the positive in each other, we will undoubtedly have a better connection. We've often seen that when we meet an outsider, we're on our best behaviour, but when we spend the entire day with them, we're more likely to detect flaws. If we can be good with others, we can be good with everyone and maintain a healthy connection.

Control of Behaviour

Individuals' behaviours or qualities differ from one another. Being completely aware of our behaviours and reactions is incredibly empowering because it allows us to make intentional choices, promote great connections, and create a more tranquil atmosphere for ourselves and others.

The purpose of wearing a watch is to do work timely. But the true meaning of life that we learn from WATCH :

W – watch your words
A – watch your actions
T – watch your thoughts
C -watch your character
H – watch your heart

Take time to respond- do not be impulsive. Taking time to respond to a situation that makes you angry or frustrated. Breathe deeply this gives you time to think. A thoughtful response reduces the chance of causing hurt. A respectful tone can convey understanding, even in tough conversations.

One little boy named Raju was conversing with his grandfather: "Inside every person, there is a battle between two wolves," the older stated.

"One of the wolves is bad. "It is anger, jealousy, greed, arrogance, resentment, lies, and ego."

"The other wolf is OK. It embodies love, peace, joy, humility, kindness, empathy, and truth.

The youngster considered for a bit before asking, "Grandfather, which wolf wins?"

His grandfather smiled and said, "The one you feed."

In times of rage, avarice, or envy, feeding the "good wolf" entails consciously choosing patience, compassion, or understanding. Similarly, when faced with the temptation to act out of fear or self-interest, we can pause and opt for courage or kindness.

Controlling conduct does not mean completely suppressing the "evil wolf"—because all emotions and urges serve a purpose. Instead, it is about cultivating the aspect of ourselves that is consistent with our values and leads to the outcomes we actually seek.

Ask yourself before making a decision, create habits, and reflect on your greater self. This helps shape who you become.

In a little, war-torn village, the only source of light at night was an antique lantern hanging in a modest inn on the outskirts of town. For years, the town had been plagued by warfare, dividing families and making neighbours afraid of one another.

Nonetheless, each evening, a bright light flowed from the inn's windows, illuminating the cobblestone roadway like a beacon of hope.

The innkeeper, an elderly man named Tomas, had lived through decades of hardship. He was a humble soul, carrying the scars of loss and pain, yet somehow he held onto a sense of kindness that was as resilient as the inn itself. Every evening, he would light the lantern and prepare a pot of hot stew, setting out loaves of bread with the hope that a weary traveller or struggling villager might find refuge. Some thought he was foolish, others thought him an idealist, but Tomas continued his ritual.

One icy winter night, a young mother named Liana and her small daughter stumbled into the inn. Their cheeks were red with cold, and their clothes were thin and worn. Tomas could see they had been traveling for days, likely escaping the devastation in the neighbouring village. Liana's eyes were downcast, her spirit visibly weighed down by grief and fear.

Without a word, Tomas wrapped his old woollen coat around her shoulders and led her and her daughter to the warmth of the fire. He ladled steaming bowls of stew and broke fresh bread, urging them to eat slowly and take their time. The little girl's face lit up as she tasted the food, and for a moment, her laughter rang out, breaking the silence of the inn. Liana watched her daughter with tear-filled eyes, the relief almost too heavy to bear.

That night, Tomas gave them a bed to sleep in, his best blankets, and a small stuffed toy—a faded, stitched bear that had once belonged to his own daughter.

Liana clutched it, her heart breaking and healing all at once, for she knew that in this stranger's act of kindness, she had found a glimmer of hope that had been missing for so long.

The next morning, Liana left the inn, vowing to carry Tomas's kindness with her. She found work in a nearby town, and with her first meagre earnings, she bought a loaf of bread and gave it to an old man on the street who looked as hungry and weary as she once had.

Months passed, and Tomas continued his nightly ritual of lighting the lantern and keeping his door open. Soon, word of his generosity spread. A soldier who had once been saved by Tomas's kindness returned to help repair the inn's roof. A baker who had once received a warm meal in his time of need started delivering fresh bread every week. Little by little, the inn became a refuge for the entire village.

Then, one spring, a terrible storm swept through the region, flooding fields, knocking down homes, and leaving many villagers without food or shelter. The people were filled with despair, feeling abandoned by fate. But as they wandered through the mud and rain, they saw the light in Tomas's inn shining brighter than ever. One by one, the villagers made their way there. Tomas, now frail and leaning on a cane, greeted each one with a smile, his eyes shining with quiet strength.

People gathered, sharing what little they had—scraps of vegetables, a handful of rice, a few potatoes. Tomas's kitchen bustled with life as everyone pitched in to prepare a simple meal. They huddled together, sharing stories, laughter, and tears.

As the storm raged outside, Tomas looked around the room, his heart swelling with pride and gratitude. He saw young and old, rich and poor, people who had once been strangers and even rivals, breaking bread together.

At that moment, Tomas knew that the goodness within each person had the power to outshine any darkness. His small acts of kindness had ignited a spark that had brought hope and unity to his village. Even in the bleakest times, people had chosen to care, to share, and to love. Tomas had always believed in the goodness of human beings, and as he looked around the room, he knew he had been right. And so, the light in Tomas's inn continued to shine, a reminder to everyone in the village that kindness could grow even in the hardest of hearts, that love and compassion could endure, and that a single lantern, lit with warmth and goodwill, could guide an entire village out of the darkness.

This story reflects the quiet heroism of everyday kindness and the goodness that often lies dormant in people until a moment calls it forth. Through the innkeeper's simple acts, we see how small gestures of compassion can kindle warmth in even the coldest of times and create lasting, positive change in the hearts of others.

Remember:

Kindness and a Compassionate Attitude are the cornerstones of humanity

Mindfulness offers a path back to balance, reminding us that the most important moment is always *now*.

Chapter : 3
Keeping Ourselves Fit And Healthy

"Health is a priceless wealth. Invest while you can."
– Bryant McGill

To operate more efficiently and effectively, we must maintain our fitness and health. To keep our bodies energetic, we must eat well, think clearly, and work hard. Maintaining fitness and health is critical for leading a healthy, meaningful life. It entails forming persistent behaviours that benefit both the body and mind.

During the growing years, an infant's body is naturally involved in a variety of activities that provide physical activity. Throughout adolescence and early adulthood, the body is healthy and active. As a result, most people keep themselves engaged with various chores such as studies or occupations, which engages both the body and mind in activities that keep them going. Nowadays, I've noticed that people are becoming more aware of the need of healthy eating habits. However, the younger generation consumes prepackaged meals, either due to a lack of time or a higher emphasis on taste. This leads to a variety of disorders that cause illness.

Regular exercise, yoga, and going to the gym are some common strategies to stay fit. The most important thing is to be conscious and make an effort. Doing and believing that you can. Consistent physical activity is vital. Muscle strengthening activities, yoga, and stretching should be included in a regular routine to increase mobility and assist prevent injuries.

When we exercise or laugh, our bodies release a hormone called endorphin. This relieves tension and is also known as the happy hormone. Endorphins are "feel-good" chemicals that the body naturally produces to help relieve pain, improve mood, and reduce stress. Sunlight exposure increases endorphin and serotonin levels, which are both mood-enhancing chemicals. Try to spend some time outside every day, even if it's just for a brief walk.

If you want to get up early in the morning, then you have to make your own decision and plan how to spend your morning hours on yourself.

The next step is to push yourself to follow a daily routine – whether it is for walking exercise or any other physical activity.

I have read someplace about ten medicines that are not available in pharmacies or principles to keep us fit and well.

• Maintain a positive outlook and tell yourself you're doing great.
• Drink enough water
• Have proper sleep
• Have a Balanced diet
• Have plenty of fruits and vegetables and natural foods
• Exercise daily, breathe in fresh air
• Love yourself
• Gratitude
• Letting go
• Early morning sunshine

Drinking Water

Water is essential for practically all human functions, including physical and mental performance, internal system regulation, and long-term health. Our bodies are composed of 70% water. It is critical to keep our bodies hydrated. It is critical for the survival of all living species, including humans. Without water, the body cannot conduct basic tasks required for survival.

Keep reminding yourself to drink water every one to two hours. Every time you drink water, feel the great energy it provides.

When the body heats up due to physical activity or external temperature, water is lost as perspiration, and drinking water refills those fluids to keep the body temperature stable. Water promotes digestion by breaking down food and allowing nutrients to be absorbed more efficiently.

We can pray to the water to keep us healthy. It heals us. We drink water to keep ourselves cool, both physically and mentally. When someone is furious, we ask them to sit down and drink some water; this simple practice helps to soothe their thoughts. Water helps us stay energized throughout the day.

Water lubricates joints, maintains muscle flexibility, and reduces the likelihood of cramping. Dehydration can cause weariness, muscle weakness, and poor coordination. Drinking water is essential for the detoxification process. Water energizes and cleans our bodies, clothing, and utensils. It provides life to our plants and animals.

Every morning, when we take a bath, send your prayers to the water to cleanse and purify our bodies both inwardly and externally. Thank the capabilities of water for all of its applications. You will experience bliss after clearing every rubbish from your body and thoughts. A positive attitude is the most effective approach to think well of yourself and others.

Importance of Breathing

Breathing is important because it reminds us that we are alive and gives us motivation to smile and accept. Every breath brings us into the present moment and nurtures our body in ways we frequently ignore. Each breath provides our bodies with oxygen, which is required for all cells to operate. Our breathing becomes faster or slower based on our emotions. Slow, deep breathing can assist to relax the nervous system, reduce anxiety, and provide a sense of tranquillity. When we meditate, we concentrate on our breath. Take deep breaths to ensure that our lungs receive adequate oxygen. Shallow, fast breathing, on the other hand, is frequently connected with anxiety and stress. When we are angry, we breathe shallowly and quickly. When you're upset, remember to take a few deep breaths before saying or doing something you'll regret later.

Breathing connects the conscious and unconscious minds. It is both voluntary and involuntary, which means we can control it when we focus on it, but it also occurs naturally. This unique duality makes it an effective tool for connecting with our inner selves, and it is used in disciplines such as yoga, meditation, and mindfulness. Every breath is a gift, a reminder of the remarkable activities that occur within us, often unseen. When we become conscious of each breath, we experience a magnificent moment of presence, life, and connection.

Mindful Eating

I've already talked about good meals and eating habits. There is much more to optimal gut health. Gut health is increasingly acknowledged as a key component of overall well-being. It contributes significantly to digestion, immunological function, mental health, and inflammation control. When our gut flora is balanced and healthy, we have better digestion, energy, mental stability, and resistance to illnesses.

Mindful eating entails being fully present throughout meals, paying attention to Flavors, textures, and sensations, and responding to hunger and fullness cues. It can aid digestion, increase satisfaction, and help you avoid overeating. This technique promotes a deeper appreciation for food, healthier, more mindful eating habits, and helps to minimize eating-related stress.
We are all aware that consuming more fibre, fewer processed and sugary meals strengthens our stomach. Fermented foods are easier to digest, thus eating more of them is advantageous. Consuming natural foods and avoiding packaged items containing preservatives.

Eat your food mindfully.
Eat slowly, using all of your senses.
Express gratitude to everyone who made the effort to offer food.
Try to keep enticing, processed meals out of sight or out of the house altogether. Stock up on healthy snacks. Have nutritious snacks on hand, such as fruits, seeds, nuts, or yogurt, so that healthier options are easily accessible.

Holistic development.

Holistic development starts with building a strong foundation of mind, body, and spirit. It is about recognizing and fostering a person's interrelated characteristics so that they might develop in a well-rounded and fulfilling manner. Holistic development considers the intellectual, emotional, physical, social, and spiritual aspects of life, striving for balance and wholeness rather than excelling in a single area. This approach understands the interconnectedness of these dimensions and the importance of balanced growth for overall success and fulfilment. Whether via faith, philosophy, or personal ideals, cultivating a sense of purpose and connection to something larger than oneself offers inner tranquillity and motivation. It also helps people discover meaning and navigate life with resilience. Development of a stress-free life, handling life challenges, and realizing one's full potential and purpose in life are all part of holistic development.

Remember :

Staying healthy and fit in mind and body is the most important aspect of living a joyful life.
Feel the energy within that is keeping you alive because every breath is a blessing.
Stay focussed and keep moving towards your goals – FOLLOW YOUR DREAMS

Chapter : 4
Embracing Growth At Any Age

Ageing is just another word for Living-
Cindy Joseph

Being and feeling young at heart is essential for living a happy, fulfilling life at any age. Staying young and appreciating every moment is the foundation for a good life.

Let the world not take you for granted or render you obsolete at any age. Growing up gracefully entails approaching each stage of life with acceptance, joy, and purpose. It is about building a mindset that prioritizes growth and wisdom above focusing exclusively on the physical changes that accompany aging.

Our bodies change, but they also reflect our life. Taking care of your body through mild exercise, adequate diet, and relaxation is critical, but so is understanding that every line and change is a sign of living completely. This method helps boost self-confidence and self-esteem. Physical activity is essential for both body and mind. Walking, yoga, swimming, or dancing can all help you feel more vibrant and energetic.

As you climb over time, you get a little out of breath, but the view is far greater - Ingrid Bergman. You get to know yourself and the life you have lived in a much better way. You get to know your purpose of life and start not only sharing your experiences but also learning from them.

At 63, I attempted to learn to swim with my daughter and granddaughter, who is just two years old. Isn't it fascinating and amusing? I'm not sure how much I could learn, but the goal was to feel good.

Feel-good factor

A positive outlook is the first step toward feeling happy. It causes a chain reaction, changing how we see obstacles and appreciate life's tiny moments. A perspective of abundance rather than scarcity promotes a sense of fulfilment. I often believe that telling our brains to be quiet, calm, and cheerful every morning results in the same feelings. But we need to remind ourselves that we must cultivate that mindset. Keep urging yourself to stay joyful.

I'm blessed.
I am peaceful.
I'm enjoying every day of my existence.

These are some of the statements that I frequently make. We can use similar statements to make ourselves feel happy.

Physical vitality frequently corresponds with emotional resilience, highlighting the importance of the body-mind relationship. Yoga, meditation, and breathwork are all effective ways to increase one's positive emotions. These techniques relax the mind, centre the emotions, and align the body, resulting in greater happiness and a sense of balance in life.

During my teaching career, I saw that some people were always upbeat and could find humour in anything. This type of person does not store things in their heart.

It may not be simple. But the ability to laugh it off and go on is the feel-good aspect that keeps them happy.

Engaging in enjoyable activities that allow one to express one's creativity, such as art, writing, music, or hobbies, fosters joy. Pursuing interests provides a sense of purpose and fulfilment, which are essential components of joyful existence. Accepting oneself as you are, with imperfections and strengths, is essential for living blissfully. Self-love is the foundation upon which other forms of happiness are built.

When my father was 89 and walking became difficult, he began writing poetry. He also read books outside of his subject area. He was an engineer, but my husband, a Chartered Accountant, gave him tax-related books. He would read and take notes in simplified language so that they could talk every morning. This was a difficult assignment, but he would complete it with the utmost honesty and willingness. This move reminds us of the need to keep ourselves as occupied as possible.

The first time I saw snowfall was very amazing for me; it made me feel so good, and I rejoiced all day, overjoyed with the realization that it was a dream come true. I took pictures and pasted them on my memory so that the blissful moments would remain unforgettable.

Beautiful moments are frequently derived from experiences rather than tangible stuff. Prioritizing experiences over goods might help us declutter our physical and emotional spaces. By focusing on what actually brings us joy and calm, we can simplify our calendars, saying no to things that do not add value to our lives and yes to those that do. Recognizing and savouring lovely events encourages thankfulness.

Gratitude can change our perspective, making us appreciate what we have rather than dwell on what we lack. A grateful attitude makes life easier by minimizing negative feelings and enhancing contentment with life as it is.

I have felt the same way since I began writing in my thankfulness journal every day: my life has become more happy. I can feel it within myself as my days get more enjoyable.

Living simply, without the relentless pursuit of worldly prosperity or superficial achievement, can result in great contentment. The "less is more" mentality encourages one to prioritize what is truly important—time with loved ones, experiences over stuff, and personal growth. Contentment is essential to feeling well because it shifts the focus from desiring more to enjoying what one already has.

When we appreciate the beauty of simplicity, we naturally make decisions that reflect a desire for a less complicated, more deliberate lifestyle. These moments remind us that life's true riches are frequently hidden in the simplest pleasures, waiting to be discovered.

Stay connected.

Social relationships offer assistance in both good and bad times. Having people to talk to, share experiences with, and seek advice from, whether they are family, friends, or members of a larger community, promotes emotional stability. This support network reduces emotions of loneliness, anxiety, and despair, resulting in a better sense of emotional well-being.

Human beings are inherently social creatures, and maintaining relationships, engaging with others, and being part of a community plays a crucial role in our mental, emotional, and even physical well-being.

Building solid relationships with loved ones and making meaningful connections will bring you joy and support throughout your life. This may entail traveling with them, paying them visits on occasion, conversing with them, and keeping up a strong connection and rapport in order to stay active and young.

Regular social interaction promotes joy and fulfilment. Positive social contacts cause an increase of endorphins, or "feel-good" hormones, which improve mood and happiness. Sharing laughter, tales, and life events with friends and loved ones fosters long-lasting memories and a sense of community.

When my father was in his late years, he would talk to old friends and coworkers, as well as relatives, which made him pleased. Staying connected has never been easier, thanks to technological improvements. Social media, video conversations, messaging applications, and online groups enable us to maintain and even develop new connections across geographic boundaries.

A simple smile, praise, or assisting someone in need not only brightens someone else's day, but it also boosts your own sense of well-being. Kindness and happiness are contagious and have a positive ripple effect, benefiting both the giver and the recipient.

Traveling

Traveling is extremely enjoyable because it exposes us to the great richness of the world in ways that no other experience can. It's not only about getting to your objective; it's about the journey itself, the encounters along the way, and how travel changes our perception of life and ourselves.

Traveling allows us to get away from our regular routines and see new cultures firsthand. We get to experience the habits, traditions, and lifestyles of individuals from all around the world. Cultural exchanges that are available whether they involve sampling local cuisine, attending festivals, or learning about their history, extend our outlook and make us more empathic and open-minded.
Traveling allows you to be in awe of the world's natural beauty. From majestic mountain ranges to serene beaches, thick forests to parched deserts, the diversity of landscapes around the world demonstrates nature's beauty and power. Standing at the base of a towering waterfall or seeing the sun rise over a tranquil lake can provide a sense of calm and a reminder of our interconnectedness with the Earth.

In this blissful journey of life, I frequently feel the need to explore new places and unwind in a setting that takes us away from our typical routines. I recall spending time with my family in Switzerland, the world's most beautiful country. I recall spending time with my family in Switzerland, the world's most beautiful country. More than the beauty of the hills or our apartment, it was the delight of being together. Whenever I feel lonely, I remember our great tour and it restores my happiness in life. Travel is more than just experiencing this particular moment; it is about making enduring memories.

Travel memories remain memorable after the journey is over, whether through images, keepsakes, or just the stories you bring back. These memories might offer both delight and nostalgia.

Traveling interrupts the monotony of daily life, allowing us to leave the familiar and go into the unknown. This adjustment in viewpoint can be both refreshing and rejuvenating. Exploring a new location frequently evokes a sense of excitement and spontaneity, which sparks creativity and inspires new ideas. It also provides opportunities for self-reflection, where we can escape from the strains of daily life and reconnect with ourselves. Traveling may be a highly personal experience. It pushes us to leave our comfort zones, adapt to new settings, and problem solve in real time. These experiences boost confidence, independence, and resilience. Whether it's navigating a foreign city or learning a few phrases in a new language, every trip contributes to our personal development, making us more adaptable and open to change.

Depending on our interests, visiting historical places, ancient structures, and museums allows us to connect with the stories of people who came before us. Walking around historic cities or viewing relics from various times helps us appreciate the legacies that have created our present. Understanding history teaches us important lessons about perseverance, culture, and progress.

It's critical to know that travel should be compatible with your physical and emotional wellbeing. If your health allows it, traveling can be a therapeutic experience that enhances overall well-being. Travel is commonly used for self-care.

Visiting a spa resort, doing yoga on a tranquil beach, or simply taking a weekend break to decompress may all rejuvenate your mind, body, and soul. Traveling can change as we get older.

Travel can be tailored to our particular requirements as we age, allowing us to appreciate the beauty and thrill of the world in more comfortable and sustainable ways. Happiness, regardless of age, is a journey that evolves. Always seek out the things that make you happy, whether they are hobbies, relationships, or interests that make you feel alive. Even in modest measures, the quest of happiness keeps the spirit alive and well.

Looking forward

Begin each day with the thinking 'I have yet to begin my adventure'. A life full of enjoyment and amusement.

You were born to blossom. Absolutely! Keeping an open mind about new enterprises, projects, and activities keeps life interesting and full of growth opportunities. Even simple activities such as going for a stroll and meeting new people can extend our ideas and provide unexpected joy or inspiration. These encounters push us beyond our comfort zones, cultivating perseverance, creativity, and a stronger connection to the world around us. Embracing the unknown, whether through big projects or small daily encounters, adds layers to our lives, fuelling a sense of purpose and curiosity.

With the grace of Divinity present in every one of us, I profoundly feel a spiritual connection, and we are incomplete without prayer. As a result, the following section discusses a few mantras that we believe make our lives easier and less stressful.

Remember :

Incorporating mindfulness into daily routines increases awareness and appreciation for life's minor joys.

- The mind is most powerful. Age is no bar to any deed.
- Maintain a positive attitude and stay involved.

CHAPTER: 5

MANTRA CHANTING

As you awaken to your divine nature, you'll begin to appreciate beauty in everything you see, touch and experience.

- Wayne Dyer

I feel that chanting Mantras is a wonderful tool for achieving your goals and connecting with God. In India, we believe in numerous gods and goddesses. However, they all point us in the direction of a more serene existence. Mantra is simply a mental technique that helps people focus, meditate, and transcend ordinary consciousness. More than simply words, they are vibrations that resonate with the universe, creating a harmonious connection and encouraging good transformation.

Chanting mantras is an ancient technique that promotes spiritual growth, mental clarity, and emotional equilibrium. Mantras, whether utilized as part of a religious rite or as a personal meditation practice, have the power to transform the mind and soul, connecting the practitioner to the divine and their true self.

In this chapter, I'd like to explain 5 fundamental mantras that we practice on a daily basis for grounding our minds, aligning our energies, and elevating our spirits. These mantras serve as tools for inner transformation, helping us connect with the divine within, embrace the present moment, and cultivate peace and positivity in every aspect of our lives.

1. OM

One of the most well-known mantras is the "Om" mantra, often referred to as the primal sound of the universe. It is considered the sound of creation and invokes a sense of unity with the cosmos. Chanting "Om" is believed to bring the practitioner into resonance with the universal vibration, promoting a sense of oneness with all existence.

Sit in a still position, close your eyes, and take a deep breath, then say OM with full reverence and concentration. Doing this daily invokes peace and serenity. This is very relaxing and removes anxiety. If it is done in a group it creates vibrations that resonate with the cosmos resulting in going deeper within yourself and forming a connection with the universe.

It helps in removing distractions if done regularly and leads to a balanced state of mind. It improves overall physical and mental health regulating the nervous system. Deep breathing strengthens the lungs and improves respiratory function. This practice can also increase oxygen supply to the body, enhancing overall vitality.

Chanting OM can create a sense of harmony between the body, mind, and spirit, leading to a more holistic and fulfilling life. Chanting OM releases endorphins, which are natural mood lifters. This practice can lead to a more positive outlook on life, reducing negative emotions like anger, jealousy, and fear. It supports the journey toward enlightenment. OM chanting is a simple yet powerful practice.

2. Gayatri Mantra

ॐ भूर्भुवः स्वः। तत्सवितुर्वरेण्यं।
भर्गो देवस्य धीमहि। धियो यो नः प्रचोदयात्॥

Om Bhur Bhuvaḥ Svaḥ
Tat Savitur Vareṇyaṃ
Bhargo Devasya Dhīmahi
Dhiyo Yo Naḥ Prachodayāt ||

Meaning: "We meditate on the divine light of the radiant source (Savitur) that pervades the three worlds: the physical, the mental, and the spiritual. May that divine light illuminate and inspire our intellect and guide us on the right path."

I remember when we were very young maybe around 8-10 years old and during our summer vacations we used to go to our grandmother's house, every night our grandmother would teach us this mantra so that we could sleep well. At that time we had learned it and it became a part of our lives. As we grew we got to know the meaning of it and continued to chant whenever we could. My mother also had formed this habit and I would watch her counting the mantra on her fingers during her walks. She told me that she did it 108 times almost every day.
We can do it as a daily practice at least 11 times 21 times or 51 times or even 108 times because these numbers have their significance.

The "Gayatri Mantra,", is one of the most revered Vedic mantras, often recited for spiritual awakening and wisdom. It is believed to invoke the sun's divine light, dispelling darkness and ignorance.

Chanting this mantra helps in sharpening the intellect and improving concentration. It clears the mind of unnecessary thoughts and enhances mental clarity.

The Gayatri Mantra is believed to create a sense of calm and inner peace. It purifies the mind and soul. It is believed to offer protection from negative energies, evil forces, and harmful influences. It helps in achieving emotional balance. The mantra invokes the divine light of wisdom, enhancing intuition and inner guidance. The vibrations of the Gayatri Mantra are said to have healing properties. They promote overall health and well-being, improving vitality and immune function. It helps in balancing and harmonizing the chakras. Regular chanting of the Gayatri Mantra fosters love, compassion, and understanding, leading to improved relationships with others.

The mantra generates positive energy and vibrations, creating a positive and uplifting environment. Chanting the Gayatri Mantra strengthens one's devotion and faith in the divine. The ultimate goal of chanting the Gayatri Mantra is to attain moksha or liberation from the cycle of birth and death. It guides the soul toward spiritual liberation and union with the divine.

I was lucky to work in a holistic environment where chanting Mantras in daily morning prayers was a common practice on all auspicious occasions.

My children have also imbibed the blessings of the Lord and as a habitual practice chant Gayatri Mantra. I was surprised one day when my 2-year-old granddaughter, who had just picked up speaking was chanting Gayatri Mantra in her baby language.

3. "Om Namah Shivaya

This is a common chant meaning I bow to Lord Shiva. Shiva is considered the destroyer of ignorance and the ego. Chanting "Om Namah Shivaya" is believed to remove negative energies, thoughts, and obstacles from one's life. The mantra is also associated with the five elements—earth, water, fire, air, and ether. Each syllable in the mantra is linked to one of these elements, symbolizing the balance and harmony of the universe.

"Om Namah Shivaya" is a deeply meaningful and powerful mantra that embodies devotion, reverence, and the quest for spiritual enlightenment. It serves as a tool for connecting with Lord Shiva and aligning oneself with the universal consciousness. In Hindu philosophy, Lord Shiva is often seen as the path to moksha or liberation from the cycle of birth and death.

4. Hare Rama Hare Rama, Rama Rama Hare Hare, Hare Krishna, Hare Krishna, Krishna Krishna Hare Hare

This mantra is also central to the International Society for Krishna Consciousness (ISKCON), founded by A.C. Bhaktivedanta Swami Prabhupada. The Mahamantra holds profound spiritual significance, and chanting it is believed to bring numerous benefits.

Both God Rama and Krishna are incarnations of Lord Vishnu. The Mahamantra can be interpreted as a call to the Lord to engage the chanter in His service and grant them spiritual upliftment and liberation. When chanted with devotion and dedication, the mantra invokes the presence of the divine in one's life, leading to a calm and serene mind, free from stress and worries. It expresses surrender to God, seeking His protection, guidance, and blessings. The repetition of the Mahamantra purifies the mind and heart, cleansing them of material desires and attachments. It helps cultivate pure devotion (bhakti) and deepens the connection with the divine.

The Mahamantra is chanted by people of diverse cultural backgrounds as a means of spiritual upliftment. In my husband's office every morning, we greet him by saying Hare Krishna. When I go for morning walks I meet many familiar faces we joyfully greet each other with "Radhe, Radhe", which is also in the praise of Lord Krishna.
It is through faith in Supreme power that we get strength by chanting and concentrating on the name of the Lord.

5. Maha Mrityunjaya Mantra

Another popular mantra is the "Maha Mrityunjaya Mantra," dedicated to Lord Shiva, which is chanted for protection, healing, and overcoming fear.

It is said to protect from negative influences and fears, including the fear of death. The mantra is believed to promote physical well-being and enhance longevity by fostering a sense of balance and harmony in the body.

Regular chanting this mantra can help calm the mind, reduce stress, and improve focus and mental clarity. It may help achieve emotional balance and reduce anxiety or depression by promoting inner peace.

Chanting the mantra is a form of spiritual practice that can help deepen one's connection with the divine and enhance spiritual awareness. It is believed to bring positive vibrations and energy into one's life, improving overall well-being. Many find these benefits valuable, experiences can vary, and it is often recommended to approach such practices with an open mind and consistent effort.

Similarly, Hindu mythology has several other mantras for different Gods and goddesses. Taking their name develops our faith and belief stronger when done consistently. Spiritual practices may be followed in different ways by different people. They all lead to contentment and peace within, understanding who you are beyond your societal roles or ego. For some people, it is a transition from a materialistic world to an inner world of happiness. It means finding emotional, mental, and even physical healing through peace, acceptance, and forgiveness.

The higher purpose of any spiritual practice is to connect with GOD. To maintain alignment with the Supreme Power and to receive His guidance. To be in harmony with all God's creations to understand the true meaning of our being, and to make this journey of life blissful.

Conclusion

As we reach the conclusion of this journey, it's important to reflect on the essence of a life well-lived—a life of simplicity, joy, health, and spiritual fulfilment. "Blissful Journey" is not merely a roadmap but a heartfelt invitation to embrace a life where stress gives way to serenity, and every moment becomes an opportunity to experience bliss.

Embracing Simplicity

Living simply does not mean living without; it means living with purpose and clarity. By simplifying our lives, we strip away the unnecessary and focus on what truly matters—relationships, experiences, and inner peace. The clutter in our homes and minds can be a source of stress, but by choosing simplicity, we make room for joy and tranquillity. Every small step towards simplicity is a step towards a stress-free life.

Relishing Beautiful Moments

Beautiful moments are the threads that weave the tapestry of a blissful life. Whether it's the first light of dawn, the laughter of a loved one, or the quietude of a starry night, these moments hold immense power. They remind us to pause, to breathe, and to be present. By cultivating an awareness of these moments, we fill our lives with gratitude and joy, creating a buffer against the pressures of modern living.

Prioritizing Health

Our well-being is the cornerstone of a joyful life. Taking care of our health—physical, mental, and emotional—allows us to live fully and vibrantly. Nourishing our bodies with wholesome foods, staying active, and getting adequate rest are essential practices. Equally important is tending to our mental health by fostering positive thoughts, reducing stress, and cultivating resilience. A healthy body and mind are the vehicles through which we experience life's beauty and pleasures.

Age as a Gateway to Joy

Age is not a barrier; it is a gateway to deeper joy and wisdom. With each passing year, we gather experiences that enrich our perspective and deepen our appreciation for life’s subtleties. Age brings the freedom to let go of societal expectations and to embrace our true selves. Joy knows no age limit, and by staying curious, active, and engaged, we ensure that every stage of life is filled with vitality and happiness.

Spiritual Growth and Faith

At the heart of a blissful journey is spiritual growth and faith. Spirituality connects us to something greater than ourselves, offering a sense of purpose and peace. It may be found in prayer, meditation, nature, or the simple act of kindness. Faith, whether in a higher power, in the goodness of humanity, or in our own abilities, provides a steady anchor in the tumult of life. It gives us the strength to pursue our dreams and the serenity to accept what we cannot change.

Fulfilling Wishes and Goals

Living a blissful life does not mean setting aside our ambitions. Instead, it means pursuing our goals with intention and joy, free from the burden of stress and fear. By aligning our desires with our values and moving forward with faith, we can achieve fulfilment without sacrificing our peace of mind. The journey towards our dreams becomes as rewarding as the realization of those dreams.

A Life of Bliss

As we conclude, remember that the blissful journey is ongoing. It is a daily practice of choosing joy over stress, simplicity over complexity, and faith over fear. By embracing the principles of simple living, cherishing each moment, caring for our health, and staying spiritually grounded, we unlock the true essence of a blissful life.
May your journey be filled with beauty, health, joy, and unwavering faith. Each day is an opportunity to live fully and blissfully. As you walk this path, remember: the blissful journey is yours to create, savour, and cherish.

Before I End Just A Few Lines Of My Poem :

BLISSFUL JOURNEY

I feel golden petals gently shower upon me,
Each moment alive with Divinity's presence.
Heaven's glitters awaken within my soul,
Their radiant glow painting smiles upon my being.

A sparkling light dances through my essence,
Its tender warmth filling each breath I take.
Every step I tread is a melody of joy,
Leading me onward along a blissful path.

This journey is mine—wholly, deeply mine,
A gift, like the sun's glow, brimming with life,
Infusing my spirit with boundless energy,
Illuminating my heart, my truth, my way.

I want to express my heartfelt gratitude to my readers once again. I feel truly blessed that this book has found its way into so many hands, bringing joy, inspiration, and light in countless ways. Your support and connection to these words mean more to me than I can ever express. Thank you for allowing this journey to touch your lives.